Breathing Spaces

Breathing Spaces

Anna Soter

Kelsay Books

Cover Art: **"Summer Morning on the Porch," 2017.**
Watercolor by Kay Bea Jones.
Professor and architect, Kay Bea Jones perceives places through sketching and painting to seek the essence of experience. She writes about modern Italian design, architecture, and urbanism, considering the social and cultural dimensions of public space. She loves prosecco, dark chocolate, and bicycling. Kay Bea Jones can be contacted at: jones.74@osu.edu

ISBN: 13-978-1-947465-31-2

Kelsay Books
Aldrich Press
www.kelsaybooks.com

Acknowledgements

Many wonderful people have helped this collection come together, have heard various poems, have come to readings, and have provided constructive feedback along the way. To single out any one individual or group would only tell part of the story of this book, but special thanks are called for, especially to those who have read and responded to many of the individual poems at various times. In particular, Terry Hermsen, Sandra Feen Diehl and the Bistro Poets, Mark Faust, Theresa Rogers, KB Jones, Chris Zacher, and Jennifer Bosveld have all, at one time or other, given challenging, insightful, and supportive feedback and critique. They enabled me to continue to think that the poems that emerged have merit, have something to say, and that some are even especially thought-provoking, and others somewhat inspirational. To every one of them, I owe deep gratitude, as well as to one of my most steadfast critics, but nevertheless greatest cheerleader—my son, Ben who has an infallible ear for rhythm and the false note.

I am also indebted to those who have invited me to read many of the poems at various poetry venues, given that those opportunities raised my awareness as to the relationship between the oral delivery of the poems and the poems on the page. For her eagle eye and unfailing sense of the poetic, I am also forever grateful to dear friend and fellow poetic traveler, Sandra Feen Diehl for also having generously given her time and effort to do a scrupulous edit of the manuscript.

Although my academic work took up much time and effort, the poetic work is what kept the creative spark going. To poetry, I ask forgiveness for having dissected you, both as a student and for many years (until I learned wisdom) as a teacher. I also thank you for your being a constant source of inspiration and rejuvenation, of reflection, and of recollection. I thank you too for being a constant companion in my life and hope that some of these poems do you justice.

For their very generous words about the collection and for being willing to have those words become what we often read first before we open the pages of a book, deepest thanks to Charlene Fix and Terry Hermsen, both superb poets and teachers of poetry.

It's not often that one has a gifted painter (K.B. Jones) as a dear friend, one who was willing to provide the perfect image that so captures the title of this collection, *Breathing Spaces*. Many wonderful hours have been "breathed" on that stone porch overlooking Iuka Ravine in Columbus, Ohio. I am honored that an image of one of her memorable paintings graces the cover of this book.

Thanks too, to the editors of the publications and venues in which the following poems first appeared:

"An Afternoon in Greenmount," displayed on the Poetry Wall, 2015, Katharine Susannah Prichards Writers' Center, Australia.

"Intimations of Immortality" in *Everything Stops and Listens* Ed. Steve Abbott, OPA Press. Mansfield, Ohio.2013, p.104.

"On a Minnesota Afternoon in August," in *Ether Arts: Literary and Visual Arts Magazine.* The Ohio State University College of Medicine, Spring, 2017.

Finally, many thanks also to Karen Kelsay, Editor of Kelsay Books, for accepting the manuscript and for her wonderful editing work in bringing this book to print.

To Ben

Contents

V

VI

VII

Nature and Nurture

Nature: The inherent quality or basic constitution of a person or thing; one's natural instincts or way of life; the physical universe; primitive state; natural state and/or scenery or environment (Merriam-Webster, 1994, p. 490).

Nurture: To care for; feed; nourish; educate, train; foster (Merriam-Webster, 1994, p. 506).

Foreword

The poems in this collection contain a medley of landscapes in which I've stood, explored, settled on, rejected, and defined one identity after another. Some echo and incorporate lines from other poems. The poems aren't arranged chronologically—as in any collage, they're arranged somewhat thematically, somewhat in relation to subject—a jigsaw puzzle. Several poems reflect my life in Australia at both ends of the continent. Most of these refer to "the bush" or "the outback."

After my family arrived in Australia, through the I.R.O. (International Refugee Organization) post W.W.II resettlement program, we were sent to the far northwest of Western Australia to a tiny town supporting blue asbestos mining until that ended in 1965. After I graduated from the University of Western Australia with a B.A. in English and Modern History, my first husband and I moved to the east, to Sydney which has remained my identified "home" in Australia—both in heart and mind. I mention the above simply to contextualize references in several poems to "bush" and "outback" life. Most of the poems reflect my years in the U.S.A—my other home.

Poetry enables an unpeeling of the self that is largely unconscious, yet ever-present even if ignored by the flesh that produces it. It calls forth the simple honesty that can emerge when the facade finally cracks, such as when a Capote character, George Whitelaw admits that he "would rather see the human wrinkles" and that "We all, sometimes, leave each other out there under the skies, and we never understand why" (Capote, T. "Mojave" in *Music for Chamelions*, p. 42). Poetry offers us an opportunity to surrender the façade.

I

*The task of art is to articulate the missing link between
the self and the world*

> Terry Hermsen, *Poetry of Place: Helping Students
> Write Their World.*

Seen Afresh on a Back Porch One Warm
Afternoon

He said, as we sat on the back porch
of my urban backyard, that god for him
exists in something as simple as women appreciating
flowers, though he can't do that—appreciate flowers
as a woman, that is, and yet he can do that
with me and with people and life in general.
And I thought how simple, and how wonderful,
expecting nothing of them, accepting that for now,
they're flowering, their seasonal shifting, being as they are
in that moment of gazing wherever that may be.
And I knew I could just let go of that baggage
that comes with being a parent, a mother in particular,
and turn new eyes on him, eyes like those women
who appreciate flowers simply for their astonishingness,
as I could with him, if I simply allow it, see him
as I see those geraniums, those petunias, those impatiens,
even the invasive honeysuckle, when it flowers.

ReWiring the Wired

I put it off and off, this going online to "update"
addresses, close accounts, confirm accounts, pay accounts,
check emails, shoulders riding all the way
to the earlobes, back stiffening

leave the desk on which the machine sits, cravings
for a cigarette marginally muted, hardly notice the draws—
the typical calming—
return, log on to my bank

scan the numbers dispassionately, even gratefully
breath fluttering, I flip through statements, note final balances
mind shifting to other avoidances, even
writing a poem for the commitment it takes

the words extracted in this moment, unwillingly.
and yet, a line appears, another spills, and another—
a sluice unlocked, words *torpedo-driven, the arrogance of tech-
whizzery*—immerse the apps-weary brain, I flow with

them, these lines to an urban backyard as we sat on a porch and
you said that God for you exists in something as simple
as women appreciating flowers, and thought of other gods—
a dog, head-lifted, neck stretched, ears butterflying

as we drove down a city street, his closed eyes
marking ecstasy, and the feverish commitment, pure drive,
pure lust for action, roars on touchdowns on any game day
during an annual August-November college football ritual

and know the line I'll deliver the next time I hear *Whaaaat?
You don't know how to use the map app?*

Gone

The house is empty now of his restless energy.
In some dorm on a campus
he discovers passion again—

had it when very young
for the rows and rows of cars
he'd line up on the steps
of the living room staircase;

for the Leggo roller coasters he'd build
on the wooden dining room floor
roller coasters we'd step around and over
for weeks, vacuum around;

he had it, despite our suppression
of spirit—we did have good intentions—
to keep him from harm,
his ardent curiosity.

Away now from our smothering concern
perhaps it will go hard for him as he learns
what we should have allowed him—to fall, to fail, to hurt,
to laugh over what we wouldn't have laughed at,

to risk, to live.

Perhaps he'll forgive us yet.

An Afternoon in Greenmount, Australia

It is a wild, romantic idea, we fall in with it, this Bloomsburyian
gentility, the women in long, floating skirts, silk draping
shirts, the men, cream boating jackets, fedoras, cravats
chest-open shirts mimicking peasants,

the poets, the artists, out with their women on this
stunning sunny day,
play croquet, cricket, clap politely,
savor the crack of a taut grape, crunch of a wafer, wrap
tongues around camembert, stilton,
finish with a Cuban – they are here
to mime another time, other poets, artists, their women.

Two of the women smoke Gauloise,
draw fiercely. It would not do to think deeply on any of it
this sun-blazed afternoon.
The other women float through yellowing grasses, swish
flies, the day's warmth climbs to heat,
damp brows melt mascara from painted faces,
they swoon heatedly, release floating, swirling
skirts, pretty draping shirts, slip stealthily, whitely, to the

reeds, to the mud in the cool dark ponds; rise, drip, dive
in the reed-edged ponds—the men dare not notice this bathing,
this cooling, these women re-emerge,
assemble floating skirts, draping shirts,
brush water from chignons, join in distant laughter,
bring cameo-selves to scones and orange-pekoe tea, score tallies,
proprietorial claims.
The men bowl, catch, count runs, drain scotch,
deal hands for bridge,
ponder the nature of art.

O'Driscoll Would Know

It was not the kind of place
you'd eulogize, evoke lovingly, this
poisoned paradise as someone once named it
blue fibers invading your every breath
red dust your every pore, yet

it permanently indented your soul
like the scar you still bear in the crook of your right elbow
a scar you earned when rounding a bend in a dry creek bed
arm flung wide as you gathered speed
evading the pretend cowboys in your game of hide and seek
when you turned your head to launch a taunt
and that arm collided with a stump of a branch left
behind when the gum tree snapped in a storm
the stump's ragged edges tearing into flesh
stopping the game, the scar forever a reminder of a time

when you hadn't lived a separated life
when you leapt into a pond twenty feet below a cliff
when you knew the taste of sweat and blood
the blood that oozed from your wounded arm
when you raced through spinifex mounds,
entangled undergrowth, spider webs strung
like wool strands on a loom, you scattering shale left and right to
be the first to reach that cliff top, sweat-drenched,
when you didn't separate mind and body
as you learned to do long after these scrambles,

now like the dust, ephemeral,
and it ruined you since, in your urbanized life
when the pendulum swung from outdoor to indoor
from leaping across hot stones, your bare feet no longer
shielded by thickened soles, to skin now softened, encased

for years in socks and shoes, so that a sliver of mulch creates
discomfort and in the keeping out of the rain, fearing the wet,
covering up from the sun, the body
losing its natural mechanism for redressing imbalances
in this now-climate-insect-controlled life, your natural defenses
shut down so that you no longer find it odd to think that birds
sucked into an aircraft's propellers should have not been in the air
in the first place—these dents too deep

to ignore so that now you're only half-alive in your cocooned
secure life away from that other world
where every moment of your existence was challenged
where your body had learned to be alert
ears to know the significance
of the slightest clatter of pebbles
nose to scent oncoming rain before clouds heralded it
gut to detect a snake just feet to your left
it ruined you because you knew what living could be
before you drifted into neutrality, into anaesthetization.

II

I wonder these (words) each morning
prise open a heart barnacled from a lifetime of competition
in marketplace thought.

Lune Variations: Pilbara Simplicity

I

Sturt pea, cardinal
garbed, adorns crumbled rock
flowers the desert.

II

Soft grass, feathered,
crowns the stealthy
spinifex.

III

Twisted mulga limbs
embrace straying sheep
under their meagre shade.

IV

A single eucalypt
leans left—windblown
cliff-top spectre.

V

Dry river bed
has known rushing water
now claims brittle skeletons.

Alleghany Rust-belt

Town after decayed town
strew the old Alleghany highway
astride the river that winds
along abandoned mines
and mills, inhabitants idled, pass time
under leaning, rotting blue porches, watch rare
tourists in search of history slow down briefly
wonder if they've left the map altogether,
wave warily, speed on to more promising destinations.
The old men nod, expect nothing more, settle
dozing white heads on chests—
an occasional Osprey
disturbs the air.

Blue Dust

The fine dust
shimmers—a chimera of clustering flecks—
fool's gold to the uninformed eye.
.

You stare at those flecks on the slides before you,
your task to tally, estimate their number per square
inch times a clever mathematical formula,
each a crocodolite fibre destined for someone's lung.

Just thirteen, they hire you, say they will train you,
manifest your dream of "Chief Surveyor"
on your future office door,
talk your father until he melts, agrees to just one year.
Pseudo-adult you ride the bus with them, the miners,
the mill-men, smoking as if you'd done it all your life,
lip-sticked lips pouting as you'd seen starlets do
in the movies, push out your budding breasts,
clinch your waist tighter, an inch to
emphasize an hour-glass shape.

You take pains for accuracy, drilling maps emerge
numbers drop on your desk telling of hours of blasting
stripping the fibrous blue mass fused into rock
walls, all endured for a chance of a better life—
five, six years, the men think and they can "go south"
these transplants from elsewhere—bring
home disaster in fibre-infused bodies,
their clothes for wives to wash,
children to hang out to dry.

You bend your head to the slides, count
them, those golden flecks as best you can, tallies of all
we'll lose twenty years down the road.

Literature and the Otherwise Indescribable

14,000 miles, 33 years later, you watched chaos
in New Orleans, Mississippi, Alabama coasts, storm
surge, levee failure, human failure, lights out, hearts out
a superdome, convention center, home now
to thousands with no homes,
cheers not even a faint memory
rapes in shadows
the living and the dead.
America wakes up.
It couldn't happen here, happened here.

You wonder if literature really makes a difference,
if living Katrina heroes read themselves in pre-storm calm,
you wonder about relevance,
if *To Kill a Mockingbird* survives in post-storm denouement,
you wonder how to say literature helps
explain the inexplicable, the indescribable
when even pastors' words sound hollow.

Intimations of Mortality

Suburbanite jungle hot-bloods
live careful lives, wait, watch,

these boys, emergent men,

catapult to adulthood
double digits signify the passage

to manhood, boil over
like milk left too long on a stove

videogaming their paths to attention
bodies strain urges to power

our belief that they're children

shredded by bullets, razed by fires
breached in trials as adults.

Note: The title of this poem is an ironic rewording of Wordworth's poem,
"Intimations of Immortality."

III

Does poetry not teach us about love, about nobility, about empathy? I knew—had long known—how poetry can break open locked chambers of possibility, restore numbed zones to feeling, recharge desire... poetry is no more, nor less necessary, than food, shelter, health, education, decent working conditions. It is as necessary.

Adrienne Rich, *What is Found There: Notebooks on Poetry and Politics.*

Beyond Moon Days

Things have a way of falling apart on moon days
you plunge
into
chopping, blending, stirring, tasting

basting, brewing, broiling, steaming,

dim the lights
bleeding
swallowing, freezing,

it was a difficult pregnancy from the start,
frying, trying,
crying,

remembering the surgeon
sweetly,
lose the sour
gratefully.

The Helpless Romantics

These survivors gather around a counter top, a blaze of
tomato reds, tawny orange of chipotle
humuus, the white of aged cheddar, purple of
grapes, bobbing yellow of quartered lemons in a pitcher,
spring-fresh skins of finely-sliced green apples
that greet them for their monthly poetic communion,
shared preoccupations, current enthusiasms,
grant reprieve from what they haven't accomplished,
as they celebrate each other's explorations into past
darknesses brought to light.

Even when wings have been clipped
they relearn to fly though one wing is shorter than the other
the desire to soar so strong
they override its influence to pilot in circles.
How can they not celebrate?

On Being Disturbed in Her Grave,[1] Emily Speaks

And would you have enjoyed being disrobed,
disturbed, however gently,
however seductively,
in the grave?
Is a woman to have no rest —
even in death—
from prying hands, tongues, eyes, limbs?

Your sleight of hand—
your feigned respect
your calling forth my sighs
a feint of hand—

I spurn your shadowed necromancy—
my love outpaces flesh—
you conjure a tamed woman
a puppet for your shadow game
masked as gentleman-y passion—

I am indeed the loaded word—
yes—"motionless" at "an open window"—
I see right through your—
"polar exploring"—my ellipses,

my "little wide-eyed glances"—
undress your false graces,
my "iceberg nakedness"—
freezes your clothed lusts.

---

[1] This poem is a response to Billy Collins' poem "Taking Off Emily Dickinson's Clothes," in Collins, B. *Sailing Around the Room: New and Selected Poems*, New York; Random House, 2001, p. 119). The words in quotation marks are cited from Collins' poem.

To a Pond: Pilbara, Australia

Under a jutting ledge above the pond
five miles from a dusty asbestos town,
a town of multiple tongues and tastes, Poles, Italians,
Hungarians, Croats to name a few.

Under that jutting ledge
five miles from this fibre-strewn town,
the pond lies darkly, silver
belly flashes its surface, rippling
a circle; a water-snake, smooth,
black, glides to the bottom of the pond.

Above that jutting ledge,
five boys, two girls, lean-limbed,
curl for the dive, curve an arc,
flash the air like kingfisher birds,
feathering, floating
the arc, slicing the pond
neatly. The hot air settles
into glossed stillness.

These Beechwold Woods, Columbus, Ohio

I ask what is the formula for this
particular white of snow in these woods
that blankets debris bruising ground
that cusps remnant, tattered leaves
that sheets these woods where
my dog and I trace others' steps.
No trimmers here
no trunks neatly hacked
trees fall of their own accord
drape each other
teeter above the ravine
some tumble half-way down
stopped in their flight only by one another
these contusions, these haphazard arrangements
somehow lovely, somehow perfect.

IV

...One of the things that makes literature something deeper and more central to us is that it speaks about us, about our lives, our choices, our emotions, our social existences, and our connections.

Martha Nussbaum, *Love's Knowledge: Essays on Philosophy and Literature.*

Night Mothering

Tonight there is no weeping, no wild stream of grief
this, a night, apacible, a night for tenderness,
for stories that your mother's pale, un-lipsticked lips
will whisper—wondrous tales
that bright-red splash of daytime lips would deny.

Day chores done, your mother tucks you in,
begins—"Once upon a time, there was a…"
recalls how you crouched when she'd raised
her hand that morning—to swipe a buzzing fly—
wondered why you'd crouched,
recalls her own mother's raised hand when she was six—
strokes now your smooth child's forehead, croons
sleep, my child for all is well this night.

Your mother not a woman for comfort,
for soothing, a woman without patience for flowers,
for the soft lies of hope—
her own story banished just like the Resurrection Lillies
she had pulled earlier this day—
those space-stealers had to go—parsnips would take their place—
now tells you stories to drift you to sleep,
of beautiful maidens rescued by golden princes,
of chivalry and pageants and castles,
her own life a story she believes not worth the telling.

You want to hear that story
as you would the story of a taken-for granted bird
that endures even the harshest winters,
that stores its fat to outlast the fiercest storms
so that it might feed and warm its young.

A Day

It was a day like most others
in a life searching for purpose, purpose
like the purpose of squirrels in the fall
leaping trunks, leaping boughs, leaping
leaves in the quest for nuts, for raining black walnuts
like the endless question why you are here
they there, what's it all about where
like endless strumming on guitars
like endless eddying at water's edge
like the salmon's leap
like the chicken laying eggs
like the rooster's crow when light
blazes, flashes on flattened horizons
as if there could be any purpose other than these
as if your purpose could be any more significant
than these endlessly repeating moments
like a mother's soothing whisper
like a father's whooping laughter
like a sister's relentless teasing
as if there were any other purpose than these.

Dualities

You are indoors, wintering, wrapped in
artificial warmth in Columbus, Ohio,
find yourself longing for the dry
bite of a winter desert wind
that needles marrow no matter how many layers,
this desert wind that you knew as you stood on a hill
above a flood-plain, trees peopling
the distance, the plain fading in the distance
becoming sky.

That wind, insistent, nagging, asserting
you will feel this, its entering your body,
demanding your attention, you huddle,
recall other knives less friendly.

A kangaroo nudges dried spinifex for a green shoot,
emus pace protectively by their young,
a hungry goanna senses alternatives.
You become one of them, no longer intruder,
their curiosity assuaged.

You merge with it—the knifing wind,
bending kangaroo, pacing emus, hungry goanna.
The silent plain settles.

No Guarantees

A new mortgage at sixty-nine is either a delusion
a perfect instance of mind over matter
or evidence that one has lost the capacity to do the math.
A thirty year mortgage, no less! Could it forestall one's
departure from the planet—this "fixed term" arrangement?

Or does it simply signal a knowing
as that of the cardinals that flit in and out of the maple
leaning over the back porch,
the squirrels' zestful late winter courtships,
the groundhog's unfailing re-emergence—
most if not every February—

that a nest is simply a nest,
that one acts according to a species-specific program,
repeats the cycle,
that it's no more nor less, to commit to thirty years
of monthly payments,
and an heir may yet benefit,
and the banks will repossess if in default,
and just as there's no guarantee one will last the distance,
there's no guarantee one won't.

Chocolate Everlasting

You might just say that you came into this life to
eat dark chocolate infused with orange essence

as much as any other reason as
your eagerness to relive your love
of milking cows, feeding calves
with a grandfather

as being a risk-taker, adventurer, go-getter, ambitious,

your "what's next, why not"
challenge
the same old answers, given
when calendars
are marked in later years
not those of long-haired days,
hipster-jean days,

jeans that clung to a lean-limbed body
through a couple of marriages
but no matter
it's
what you can't reduce, discard,
mark with price-tags, attach as a feather to your cap.
the reason you take to the grave.

V

And poetry is ... the crossing of trajectories of two (or more) elements that might not otherwise have known simultaneity.

Adrienne Rich, *What is Found There: Notebooks on Poetry and Politics.*

Ordinary Rituals

The squirrels' instinctive chasings up and down bare maples,
the sweep of a hawk in pursuit of prey,
the gleam of ice still crusting soil and stones in the ravine,
the regular-as-sunset strut of the orange tomcat
that established territory on the back patio,
remind that this is where magic always lies if absent elsewhere,
that these miracles happen
regardless of which politician vilifies another,
who is fired, who is reinstated,
which laws rescinded or not,
in the tug of wars between egos and egos,
remind us that these daily rituals, are ever-enacted,
intuitively lived, and that the cat will lick
its strong orange paws when it has strutted its path,
the hawk will seek another prey,
the squirrels repeat their dance on one or other bare maple,
the ice will become water and water will become ice,
whether you or I attend or not.

Dog Lives the Moment

He stands, tip-toed, cranes forward,
dog elbows rest on the car window,
head lifts, neck stretches, ears butterfly
as we drive down High Street, Columbus,
closed eyes suggest ecstasy—dog nirvana—
without a single course in meditation,
without a single word on mindful presence.

It has taken me a lifetime to achieve
glimpses of his state—he
simply leans out of an open car window.

A Garden's Counterpoint

That late summer, you pulled the Resurrection Lilies,
their bulbs deep-buried, space-stealers.
They had to go.

That same week in your former workplace,
two deaths announced untimely loss,
one a colleague's father,
another, a friend's brother.
You regret pulling the lilies.

The hostas, sun-bleached, drop
leaf after leaf though you urged them
to last with extra watering,
they and their white-flaring flowers.

The following week you hear of a raging man in New York
who shot another, he too, claimed by bullets
in the aftermath.

You submit, allow the roses and day lilies seasonal departure,
escape pruning shears, relocation, this time—
the petunias, impatiens,
outlasting them all.

Random Lines on an Afternoon

The dog and I will walk soon,
he to sniff grass blades knifing up the sidewalk,
I move to empathy, the believing game
that we mostly try our best
choose to stay, a loved child the choice for duration,
choose to not read those magazines
that tell women how to please their men,
practice belief that a date on a calendar's just an invention,
time an invention,
wonder who dropped the envelope,
its spine marked by a sneaker's tread,
recall framed villages mimicking life to come,
wonder the power of a sketch—
the dog stretches delicate limbs, flutters eyelids,
senses possibilities, accepts the leash.

On Any Saturday in the Fall

Any home-game day during the annual
August through November ritual
a scene repeated all over the Ohio valley
where alumni and fans relive their brush with glory
faces shining anticipation

streaming scarlet and grey, buckeye-beaded,
rhinestone-edged "Big OH" caps bob and nod
in the mom and pop cafes, the Bob Evanses,
Harry's Hearty Breakfast Bars, countless others
offer plates loaded with maple-syrup-doused
pancakes, sugar-sprinkled toast,
sturdy bacon slices, glistening sausages,
the trendier sites, self-declared healthier versions
of the same stokings for the ups and downs,
the chantings on a Saturday during College football season,
the touchdown roars, the deep sighs,
groans, silences of lesser moments in the game.

One needs stoking breakfasts for such
events, the energy palpable, calories evaporating
in feverish commitment. In its finest form,
this is innocent of guile,
just pure drive, pure lust for action,
for whatever pinnacle can be reached
in those few hours
on any Saturday in the Fall.

VI

It's about hope, fruitfulness, possibilities.

Movie Manouvres

You are reminded to bring umbrellas
Saturday night, movie night in this outback
mining town, the roofless cinema promising
weekly escape, surprise downpours,
a chance to flirt with the local boys,
your hair, a spray-frame
masking anticipation.

Light flickers on the screen
casts imagined sophistication
hands seek hands as cowboys strut,
guns on hips slung low,
teeth bared to snarl their challenge,
lips meet lips, tongues probe,
disrupt the night. The gunman
draws, spits, a second's hesitation
leaves him in the dust, smoke cools
from the hero's pistols, credits reel,
hands, tongues, lips retreat,
passion holstered for another week.

Raccoon Reading Indifference

Past week's living history
marks your passage up 8th Avenue,
you wonder who dropped the envelope,
its spine marked by a sneaker's tread,

wonder what was in that letter,
if the wearer of the mud-splattered white t-shirt
still damp from night's dew,
went home naked,

wonder if the guy who propped
a drained vodka bottle
in the bleached grass on the curb corner
made it to a bed last night.

A raccoon, creature of urban nights,
miniature refuse truck,
travels the alleys, scales the dumpsters,
goldmines of indifference,

knows the spoils of waste,
the bland-faced wrist-fling of an Arby's wrapper.

A Brief Encounter

A gas station attendant, he
looks up from the cash register
when queried where he's been lately
surprise creasing his face, eyebrows lifting,
then a smile, the line behind me becoming restive,
but he has nimble fingers, a multi-tasking mind,
draws out my change, thanks me for asking

that small thing "Where have you been lately?"
He says he's transferring,
doesn't know where yet, but he'll tell me—
if I come by again the next day
so I can fuel up there, at his new outlet,
so I can ask him again, then, how he is, on that day,
so he will be acknowledged as someone to notice,
more than a body behind a cash register,
more than a functionary, his smile
reaching his eyes.

First Lines

I wonder these each morning
        prise open a heart barnacled

from a lifetime of competition in marketplace thought.
        He calls from an emergency room - chest pains, he says.

She walks the dusty road spotted with other women's blood.
        I loved you dearly, the song goes.

This year I've deleted seasons—the ones marked in the calendar,
        past week's living history marks our passage up 8th Avenue.

Back then, in dusty heat and flies, she sketched New England
        towns, drank coffee, licked ice-cream at a country café.

Last Lines

Have that back-porch coffee and smoke - let go of anything
        mattering more, well-intentioned parents, partners, lovers,
        friends, doing our best.

Where you once stood—she's now there. You wonder
        how to beautify to satisfy, how to remain interesting,
        alluring.

The dog simply leans out of an open car window
        manifests belief that a date on a calendar's just an
        invention, time an invention.

You wave your trash bag, your picker, you grin.
        wonder the power of care.

On a Minnesota Afternoon in August

You could be anywhere, but you aren't, and really,
it can only happen on the shores of this particular lake
in northern Minnesota, where the light
mutes the jaggedness of this time
the lake's calm measuring yours.

Those years professoring a crown
you no longer need if you ever did—
those students, those colleagues, with whom
you held your own
your knowing sidereal grace,
your tempered kindnesses
fed each day by a loving wife, family,
your dogs determined to last you out—
fear has fled where it cannot roost
you call to us as the loons do
nudging us to the lake's open waters,
you circle our peripheries.

Someone nearby flings, casually, a flat blue stone
that skips its tune across the pond
an old child's game that draws your quiet smile—
paling leaves drift to forest floor
begin the autumnal cycle
Lady's Slipper petals, rain-drenched, spiral droplets —
the earth, and you, quiver quiet attention.

The loons hoot to gather their chicks
chorus retreat
from grassy banks
afternoon stillness restored.

VII

If I have been a good parent to the poem,
something will happen to you who read (or hear) it.

Adrienne Rich, *What is Found There:*
Notebooks on Poetry and Politics.

Parallel Realities

Spring buds the maples, calls crocuses to flower
nudges grass to waken, feathered green shoots
edge through deadened winter yellows.

Cardinals, bluejays prepare love songs
dance still-bare branches
scavange materials for nesting.

Indoors, children slump over sleek screens,
servants to their finger-tips,
play the machines sunrise to sunset.
Seasons come and go, they click days away.

Ephemera

We meet, discuss a merger
deliberate alignments
a doctoral student's dissertation stalls
others defer candidacy for a first child
an ill parent.

We intone, debate, take notes
who is teaching what, publishing where,
estimate national rankings, measure significances
according to where, what, and when published.

One sits in a dusty office, writing, content,
another wonders why he slips in and out
of sleep all day, body barometer muted.

We surge from one meeting to another
a student is tired, chooses diesel for a gas engine
the car needs towing;
a secretary wonders how she'll make ends meet
considers extra work in a laundromat
to pay son's medical bills.

We talk targeted investments
who shall survive
who shall thrive
who shall rise
from anonimity

We scramble to present our
shinier selves.

The Real World According to Newspapers

One hundred and seventy-two die in attacks by Iraqui rebels,
Mad Cow disease strikes—industry too lax, critics complain,
Iranian earthquake death toll twenty thousand and rising,
holidays declared bleak for workers at major grocery chain.

We meet for breakfast, you and I, our usual place, the Sunday
headlines counterpointing our talk of chores, love,
your five-year old's drawing of his first picture for you.

Headlines declare US Homeland Security is a business bonanza,
the Pakistani president's not lacking for enemies,
Afghan fighting goes on … and on …
modeling tot's mother sues city over playground injuries,
three snowboarders feared missing, possibly dead after avalanche
strikes.

We read lines brought to share—
our media-reality antidotes—
Mary Oliver's "Morning Poem" with
its "heaps of ashes of the night/turn(ed) into leaves again,[2]"
Doug Gray's "dining room (where) the
"ice cubes melt over lemon slices.[3]"
This poetry as good as any prayer.

.

[2] Oliver, Mary. "Morning Poem," in Dream Work,. New York: Atlantic Monthly Press. 1986, p.6.
[3] Gray, Douglas. "Some Blue Hotel," in Words on the Moon.. Minneapolis, MN: Mid-List Press, 1993, p. 68.

It's Not About the Alphabet

A stolid, sweaty figure in this town of red dust, blue dust,
you leaned toward your reluctant charges
reciting "A.B.C.," and we followed stumblingly,
preferring to dream not of "a" as in "cat" or "b" as in "box"
but of the glass marbles abandoned near a woodpile,
the schoolyard tree that invited climbing,
the recess skipping contests,
the after-school scattering to that first crossing rock pool,
where we competed with tadpoles for the deepest dives.

How frustrated you must have been
sent to teach the alphabet to we outback kids in what
you thought a god-forsaken hamlet in a Mars-like landscape
over a thousand miles from what you defined as "civilization"
your charges feeling your anger, finding you spiteful as you,
then unsmiling, ground us to your dust of words on paper.

And yet you are recalled, your angular form, your persistent
enunciation of every vowel and consonant, for now I think
of you as human, as woman, as lonely when you withdrew
to your simple barren hut (so like ours) each night,
and how intolerable it must have been back then, your
distaste for pervasive dust, endless heat, isolation
from all you held dear, overriding your capacity for love.

Survivors

She waves as we drive past her heat-shimmering
shack that shakes with cats, reeks of cats, keens with cats.
"Come on in," she calls, "I've baked some scones, a cake—
don't mind the cats!" Dorothea, Outback Duchess,
ex-Prussian countess (so she says), married
an English coal miner after "the" war,
came in a migrant ship for a better life (so she says).

Across the creek, Old Frannie, thread-thin, bore nine children,
reared them in the heat of the north, on the edge of a desert,
husband long departed, struggles to make ends meet,
creates a legacy of cunning thrift, this local junk-yard mistress,
builds her mounds of empty beer bottles, rusted pots and pans,
broken chairs and chests.

One loved by and loving cats,
floats airs and graces, afternoon-tea charades,
the other stakes her claim on other people's cast-offs,
they, storm-beaten cliff-faces,
the call of the wild, the indestructibles.

,

About the Author

Following her early years in the Austrian Alps where she was born, Anna grew up in the Australian northwest region (The Pilbara), and lived for most of her adult life in Sydney, prior to undertaking a Ph.D. specializing in applied linguistics and language pedagogy in the USA. She is Professor Emeritus at The Ohio State University (OSU), Columbus, Ohio having taught in the English Education program there between 1986-2012, as Professor Emeritus, she continues to teach, mentor, and write through her roles as Faculty Mentor in the STEP Program, Co-Chair of the OSU Medicine and the Arts Roundtable Board, and serves as faculty editorial advisor of the Humanism in Medicine literary magazine, *Ether Arts*. She is also Adjunct Professor in the School of Education and Health Sciences at Murdoch University (Australia), Adjunct Professor at Self-Design Graduate Institute (Bellingham, USA), and Adjunct Faculty at the Columbus College of Art andDesign (CCAD). For the past ten years, she has been exploring and writing about intersections between the literary arts (especially poetry) and the field of health and wellbeing.

Anna is Founder (2010) and current co-chair with Fred Andrle and Charlene Fix of *The Hospital Poets US Program* for The Ohio State University Medicine and the Arts Program/Humanism in Medicine. Since 2010, she also created and provided monthly *Poetry & Writing for Wellbeing Workshops for the JamesCare for Life Cancer Survivorship Program*. In 2016, she launched *Hospital Poets Australia* in collaboration with the Katherine Susannah Prichard Writers' Center, Perth, Australia. She has been a featured reader in venues in Ohio and her poetry has been published in various magazines and anthologies. Anna recently returned to the US, following an extended stay in Australia.

She can be contacted at
soter.1@osu.edu, or annasoter@aol.com.